JESUS
Is My All in All

DOUBLEDAY

New York   London   Toronto   Sydney   Auckland

JESUS
Is My All in All

✳

*Praying with
the "Saint of Calcutta"*

MOTHER TERESA

Edited and introduced by
Fr. Brian Kolodiejchuk, M.C.

Imprimi potest: Robert Conroy, M.C., Superior General
Nihil Obstat: Msgr. Michael F. Hull, S.T.D., Censor Librorum
Imprimatur: † Dennis J. Sullivan, D.D., Vicar General,
Archdiocese of New York
March 24, 2008

The *Nihil Obstat* and *Imprimatur* are official declarations that a book or pamphlet
is free of doctrinal or moral error. No implication is contained therein that
those who have granted the *Nihil Obstat* and the *Imprimatur* agree with the
content, opinions, or statements expressed.

DOUBLEDAY

PUBLISHED BY DOUBLEDAY

Published in the United States by Doubleday, an imprint of The Doubleday
Publishing Group, a division of Random House, Inc., New York.
www.doubleday.com

A previous edition was privately published by The Mother Teresa Center
in 2005. Copyright © 2005 by The Mother Teresa Center.

DOUBLEDAY is a registered trademark and the DD colophon
is a trademark of Random House, Inc.

Photo credits appear on page 51.

Book design by Maria Carella

Cataloging-in-Publication Data is on file with the Library of Congress.

ISBN 978-0-385-52725-5

1 3 5 7 9 10 8 6 4 2

First Edition

CONTENTS

PREFACE

This is a revised version of the novena that was originally prepared to commemorate the first celebration of Blessed Teresa of Calcutta's feast on 5 September 2004.

The following novena is composed from the words of Mother Teresa. Allowing her message and example to penetrate our hearts prayerfully is essential to commemorating her life and holiness. Meditating on Mother Teresa's simple yet profound teaching can help us to grow in our own love and thirst for Jesus and teach us how to love and to serve as she did: "All for Jesus through Mary" by doing "small things with great love."

Not only do we have the rich inheritance of Mother Teresa's words and example to inspire us, but we also have the solace of her ongoing concern for each one of us and the assistance of her constant intercession. Herein is the beauty and wonder of the communion of saints: while we look to Mother Teresa's exemplary life for inspiration, we receive at the same time the blessings of her prayer for our needs and intentions.

May Mother Teresa's way of holiness be a light to each one of us, bearing fruit in our own desire for holiness and in our joyful service of Jesus present in all our brothers and sisters, especially those most in need.

Fr. Brian Kolodiejchuk, M.C.
Postulator, Cause of Canonization
Director, Mother Teresa Center

JESUS
Is My All in All

INTRODUCTION

MOTHER TERESA'S CALL

Gonxha Bojaxhiu, the future Mother Teresa of Calcutta, was born in Skopje on 26 August 1910. At the age of eighteen, she traveled to Ireland to join the Institute of the Blessed Virgin Mary (commonly known as the Loreto Sisters). After a few weeks in Ireland, Gonxha—now known as Sister Teresa—was sent to India, where she made her first profession of vows in 1931 and final profession in 1937. She spent eighteen years at the Loreto School in Calcutta, first as a teacher and later also as headmistress.

On 10 September 1946, during a train ride from Calcutta to Darjeeling, Mother Teresa received an "inspiration," which she later described as a "call within a call." Jesus's thirst for love and for souls became so distinctively clear that from then on an ardent longing to satiate His thirst took complete possession of her heart. By means of interior locutions and visions, Jesus revealed to her the desire of His Heart for "victims of love" who would "radiate His love on souls." He revealed His pain at the way the poor were neglected, His sorrow at their ignorance of Him, and His longing—His thirst—for their love. He pleaded with her: "My little one—come—come—carry Me into the holes of the poor.—Come be My light.—I cannot go alone—they don't know Me—so they don't want Me. You come—go amongst them, carry Me with you into them.—How I long to enter their holes—their dark unhappy homes."

Jesus asked Mother Teresa to start the Missionaries of Charity, a religious community dedicated to the service of the poorest of the poor. The Society of the Missionaries of Charity was officially established in the Archdiocese of Calcutta on 7 October 1950.

Mother Teresa's whole life and labor reflected the joy of loving God and neighbor, especially those most in need, the poorest of the poor. Her response to Jesus's plea ("Come, be My light") made her a symbol of compassion in the world and a living witness to the love of God. Her life showed the world the greatness and dignity of every human person, the value of little things done faithfully and with great love, and the inestimable worth of intimate union with God.

On 5 September 1997, Mother Teresa's earthly life came to an end. Two days later, Pope John Paul II described her in this way: "I have a vivid memory of her diminutive figure, bent over by a life spent in service to the poorest of the poor, but always filled with inexhaustible interior energy: the energy of Christ's love. Missionary of Charity: this is what Mother Teresa was in name and in fact."

Indeed, her mission of charity and great reputation of holiness drew vast crowds to her funeral, and her tomb immediately became a pilgrim site and a place of prayer for people of all backgrounds, creeds, and social classes.

Just six years after her death, Pope John Paul II beatified Mother Teresa in St. Peter's Square on

19 October 2003. In his address to the pilgrims, the Holy Father referred to her as "one of the greatest missionaries of the twentieth century." The Pope emphasized that it was her relationship with God, nourished by prayer, that inspired all her undertakings and made her mission so fruitful in the world. At the very heart of this intimate relationship with God were the words of Jesus on the Cross: "I thirst" (John 19:28). "Satiating Jesus's thirst for love and for souls in union with Mary, the Mother of Jesus," said the Pope, "had become the

sole aim of Mother Teresa's existence and the inner force that drew her out of herself and made her 'run in haste' across the globe to labor for the salvation and the sanctification of the poorest of the poor."

Her choice to humbly serve the poorest of the poor made the Gospel of Love come to life. With her words and actions, Mother Teresa touched the hearts of believers and nonbelievers alike, crossing the barriers of class, religion, culture, and nationality. Her life became a sign that "God still loves the world today." Her secret was simple: she allowed Jesus to take full possession of her life so that He could act in her and through her.

Jesus Is My Everything

Mother Teresa's spiritual director, Jesuit Father Céleste Van Exem, said of her: "The meaning of her whole life was a person: Jesus." Indeed, for Mother Teresa, Jesus was everything. When asked by a reporter, "Mother, what place do you give to Jesus in your life?" she immediately replied, "I give Him *all the place*." This total belonging to Jesus is evident in the following meditation that Mother Teresa composed while hospitalized in Rome in 1983.

"WHO DO YOU SAY THAT I AM?"
(Matthew 16:15)

You are God.

You are God from God.

You are Begotten, not made.

You are One in Substance with the Father.

You are the Son of the Living God.

You are the Second Person of the Blessed Trinity.

You are One with the Father.

You are in the Father from the beginning:

All things were made by You and the Father.

You are the Beloved Son in Whom the

Father is well pleased.

You are the Son of Mary,

Conceived by the Holy Spirit in the womb of

  Mary.

You were born in Bethlehem.

You were wrapped in swaddling clothes by Mary

And put in the manger full of straw.

You were kept warm by the breath of the donkey
That carried Your mother with You in her womb.
You are the Son of Joseph,
The Carpenter, as known by the people of
    Nazareth.
You are an ordinary man without much learning,
As judged by the learned people of Israel.

WHO IS JESUS TO ME?

Jesus is the Word made Flesh.
Jesus is the Bread of Life.
Jesus is the Victim offered for our sins on the
    Cross.

Jesus is the Sacrifice offered at the Holy Mass
For the sins of the world and mine.
Jesus is the Word—to be spoken.
Jesus is the Truth—to be told.
Jesus is the Way—to be walked.
Jesus is the Light—to be lit.
Jesus is the Life—to be lived.
Jesus is the Love—to be loved.
Jesus is the Joy—to be shared.
Jesus is the Sacrifice—to be offered.
Jesus is the Peace—to be given.
Jesus is the Bread of Life—to be eaten.
Jesus is the Hungry—to be fed.
Jesus is the Thirsty—to be satiated.
Jesus is the Naked—to be clothed.
Jesus is the Homeless—to be taken in.
Jesus is the Sick—to be healed.
Jesus is the Lonely—to be loved.
Jesus is the Unwanted—to be wanted.
Jesus is the Leper—to wash his wounds.
Jesus is the Beggar—to give him a smile.
Jesus is the Drunkard—to listen to him.

Jesus is the Retarded—to protect him.

Jesus is the Little One—to embrace him.

Jesus is the Blind—to lead him.

Jesus is the Dumb—to speak for him.

Jesus is the Crippled—to walk with him.

Jesus is the Drug Addict—to befriend him.

Jesus is the Prostitute—to remove from danger
    and befriend.

Jesus is the Prisoner—to be visited.

Jesus is the Old—to be served.

To me—

Jesus is my God.

Jesus is my Spouse.

Jesus is my Life.

Jesus is my only Love.

Jesus is my All in All.

Jesus is my Everything.

Jesus, I love with my whole heart, with my whole
being. I have given Him all, even my sins, and He
has espoused me to Himself in tenderness and love.

Now and for life I am the spouse of my Crucified Spouse. Amen.

Jesus, the Light to Be Lit

Mother Teresa once assured her followers, "Mother is here to help you, guide you, lead you to Jesus. Time is coming closer when Mother also has to go to God. Then Mother will be able to help each one of you more, guide you more, and obtain more graces for you."

Mother Teresa's mission to guide us to Jesus's light and to help each of us "be His light" still continues. What she wrote years ago is realized even more effectively today as she intercedes for us from Heaven: "I pray that each one of you be holy, and so spread His love everywhere you go. Light His Light of truth in every person's life, so that God can continue loving the world through you and me."

Be only all for
Jesus
through Mary
Be holy.

God bless you
M. Teresa mc

THE NOVENA

A novena (derived from the Latin word *novem,* meaning "nine") is a traditional Catholic devotion in which public or private prayer is offered on nine consecutive days for a particular need or intention or in preparation to celebrate a special feast (for example, Christmas, Pentecost, the Feast of Divine Mercy). The first novena took place in the upper room in Jerusalem after Jesus had ascended into Heaven, when the apostles "with one accord devoted themselves to prayer, together with the women and Mary the mother of Jesus, and with his brethren" (Acts 1:14) as they awaited the coming of the Holy Spirit on the day of Pentecost. Since the seventeenth century, numerous novenas addressed to God, to the Blessed Virgin Mary, or to one of the saints have been composed; novenas to the Sacred Heart, to Our Lady, and to St. Joseph, St. Jude, and St. Thérèse of Lisieux are popular examples. We pray to the saints in Heaven, and they, being closer to God than we on earth, intercede with Him for our needs.

Thus, everyone is welcomed to pray a novena to any of God's faithful servants. Our Heavenly Father, who commands us to "love one another" (John 13:34), is pleased to answer the prayers of His children in Heaven who petition Him for the needs and concerns of their brothers and sisters on earth.

It should be emphasized that a novena is not a magic formula and should not become a superstitious practice. Prayer always presupposes faith, humility, and dependence on God and His divine will. Thus, the novena could also become nine days of practicing a greater openness to the will of God and ultimately of learning to surrender to His providential designs. It should also be remembered that, "according to Scripture, it is the heart that prays. If our heart is far from God, the words of prayer are in vain" (*Catechism of the Catholic Church*, 2562).

FAVORS RECEIVED
THROUGH THE NOVENA

The experiences of those who already have prayed this novena provide examples of the possible fruits of praying the novena and serve as encouragement to turn to God by seeking Mother Teresa's prayers in the many needs that arise daily.

"One friend of mine . . . had a cross to bear when her husband left without a word. . . . She began to pray [the novena to Mother Teresa]. On the ninth day he returned home. . . . Everything came out in the open and a beautiful healing has taken place."

"I am so thankful for the novena you have prepared, and assure you that it is a comfort to hear Mother Teresa's words, not only to help us in our trials but to redirect our thoughts to God and satiating His thirst. It has meant more to me than you know."

Favors reported by those who have prayed this novena have been many. One grace consistently mentioned is that of experiencing a greater closeness to God. Mother Teresa, now in Heaven, is ever faithful to her mission to bring souls to God and God to souls.

God Speaks in Silence

Before beginning, seek a silent place that will help you to pray, preferably in a church or chapel in front of the Blessed Sacrament. Create silence within yourself, for "God is the friend of silence." He is always waiting for us in silence—to speak to us and to listen to us. "In the silence of our hearts, God speaks of His love; with our silence, we allow Jesus to love us" (Mother Teresa).

Read some or all of the quotes provided for the day and allow them to penetrate your heart. Stay with Mother Teresa's words for a while and let one of the thoughts grow in your heart and accompany you throughout the day. Unite yourself with all your brothers and sisters throughout the world who are suffering in darkness and pain, then prayerfully recite the "Prayer to Blessed Teresa." You may also make some concrete act of charity toward someone in your own family, community, or neighborhood as a way of living more profoundly the spirit and message of Mother Teresa during the novena.

OVERVIEW

The first day of the novena is dedicated to knowing Jesus, the wellspring of Mother Teresa's life and mission.

On the second day, we are invited to believe in the unconditional love that Jesus has for each of us. It was this faith in His love that prompted Blessed Teresa to leave her family and homeland, and to set out for the missions.

On the third day, Jesus invites us through Blessed Teresa to go in spirit to Calvary and hear Him say to us from the Cross: "I thirst." This was the inner fire that consumed the heart of Blessed Teresa.

The fourth day is dedicated to Our Lady, who

will help us to better understand the thirsting love of Jesus and to respond to it as she did: with loving trust, total surrender, and joy. Therefore, the fifth, sixth, and seventh days are dedicated to these three dispositions of the heart: trust, total surrender, and joy, respectively.

On the eighth day, we are invited to enter into the mysteries of Jesus's presence in the Eucharist and in the poor. We, too, are called to receive Jesus in the Bread of Life, to be transformed into Him and to serve Him in the poorest of the poor. As Mother Teresa so often explained, "We serve Him by doing to them [the poor] what we would like to do to Him. Here is the sanctity hidden for us—in knowing Jesus, loving Jesus, serving Jesus."

The ninth day is dedicated to the call to sanctity through knowing and serving Jesus in the poorest of the poor.

Prayer to
Blessed Teresa of Calcutta

Blessed Teresa of Calcutta, you allowed the thirsting love of Jesus on the Cross to become a living flame within you, and so became the light of His love to all. Obtain from the Heart of Jesus (*here make your request*). Teach me to allow Jesus to penetrate and possess my whole being so completely that my life, too, may radiate His light and love to others. Amen.

Immaculate Heart of Mary, Cause of Our Joy, pray for me.

Blessed Teresa of Calcutta, pray for me.

First Day:
Know the Living Jesus

"Deep down in every human heart there is a knowledge of God. And deep down in every human heart there is the desire to communicate with Him."

"The more we know God, the more we will trust God."

"We must know God, that God is love, that He loves us, and that He has created us—each one of us—for greater things. He has created us to love and to be loved."

"Do you really know the living Jesus—not from books but from being with Him in your heart?"

"Am I convinced of Christ's love for me and mine

for Him?…What must we do to get this conviction? We must know Jesus, love Jesus, serve Jesus. Knowledge will make you strong as death. We know Jesus through faith: by meditating on His Word in the Scriptures, by listening to Him speak through His Church, and through the intimate union of prayer."

THOUGHT FOR THE DAY:
Don't search for Jesus in far lands; He is not there. He is close to you; He is in you.

Ask for the grace of an intimate knowledge of Jesus.

Recite the "Prayer to Blessed Teresa," found on page 21.

Second Day:

Jesus Loves You

"The personal love Christ has for you is infinite."

"You are special to God. . . . He is waiting for you to come to Him in prayer. He wants to honor you by filling you with His Presence."

"What does it mean to be alone with Jesus? It doesn't mean to sit alone with your own thoughts. . . . It means that you know that He is close to you, that He loves you, that you are precious to Him, that He is in love with you. He has called you, and you belong to Him. If you know that . . . you will be able to face any failure, any humiliation, any suffering— if you realize Jesus's personal love for you and yours for Him."

"The devil may try to use hurts of life, and sometimes our own mistakes, to make you feel it is impossible that Jesus really loves you, is really cleaving to you. This is a danger for all of us. And so sad, because it is completely opposite of what Jesus is really wanting, waiting to tell you.... He loves you always, even when you don't feel worthy."

"Jesus loves you tenderly, you are precious to Him. Turn to Jesus with great trust and allow yourself to be loved by Him."

THOUGHT FOR THE DAY:
Do not be afraid—you are precious to Jesus. He loves you.

Ask for the grace to be convinced of Jesus's unconditional and personal love for you.

Recite the "Prayer to Blessed Teresa."

Third Day:

Hear Him Say to You: "I Thirst"

"In His agony, in His pain, in His loneliness, He said very clearly, 'Why have You forsaken Me?' He was so terribly lonely and forsaken and suffering on the Cross.... At this most difficult time He proclaimed: 'I thirst.'... And the people thought He was thirsty in an ordinary way and they gave Him vinegar straight-away; but it was not that He thirsted for—it was for our love, our affection, that intimate attachment to Him, and that sharing of His passion. And it is strange that He used such a word. He used 'I thirst' instead of 'Give Me your love.'... The thirst of Jesus on the Cross is not imagination. It was a word: 'I thirst.' Let us hear Him saying it to me and saying it to you.... It is really a gift of God."

"If you listen with your heart, you will hear, you will understand. . . . Until you know deep inside that Jesus thirsts for you, you can't begin to know who He wants to be for you. Or who He wants you to be for Him."

"Follow His footsteps in search of souls. Carry Him and His light into the homes of the poor, especially to the souls most in need. Spread the charity of His Heart wherever you go and so satiate His thirst for souls."

THOUGHT FOR THE DAY:
Just think! God is thirsting for you and me to come forward to satiate His thirst.

Ask for the grace to understand Jesus's cry of thirst.

Recite the "Prayer to Blessed Teresa."

Fourth Day:
Our Lady Will Help You

"How much we need Mary to teach us what it means to satiate God's Thirsting Love for us, which Jesus came to reveal to us. She did it so beautifully. Yes, Mary allowed God to take possession of her life by her purity, her humility, and her faithful love.... Let us seek to grow, under the guidance of our Heavenly Mother, in these three important interior attitudes of soul that delight the Heart of God and enable Him to unite Himself to us, in and through Jesus, in the power of the Holy Spirit. It is in doing so that, like Mary our Mother, we will allow God to take full possession of our whole being—and through us God will be able to reach out His Thirsting Love to all we come in contact with, especially the poor."

"If we stand with Our Lady, she will give us her spirit of loving trust, total surrender, and cheerfulness."

THOUGHT FOR THE DAY:

How close we must keep to Our Lady who understood what depth of Divine Love was being revealed as she stood at the foot of the Cross and heard Jesus cry out: "I thirst."

Ask for the grace to learn from Our Lady to quench Jesus's thirst as she did.

Recite the "Prayer to Blessed Teresa."

Fifth Day:
Trust Jesus Blindly

"Trust in the good God, who loves us, who cares for us, who sees all, knows all, can do all things for my good and the good of souls."

"Christ accepted to die because He trusted His Father. He knew that from that apparent failure God will work out His plan of salvation. For us, too, we must have that deep faith and trust that if we are doing God's will, He will work out His plan of salvation in us and through us in spite of any failure we may meet."

"Jesus never changes....Trust Him lovingly, trust Him with a big smile, always believing He is the

Way to the Father, He is the light in this world of darkness."

"So let us all make that one strong resolution that we will be all love to Jesus in the world...that we will be at His disposal to make use of us without consulting us. And I think that is the best way to show our love for Him, to accept Him as He comes. If He wants to come into our life in humiliation, in suffering, all right; if He wants in publicity, all right. Whatever it be, success, failure, it makes no difference to Him, and it should not make a difference to us either."

"Mary, too, showed that complete trust in God by accepting to be used for His plan of salvation in spite of her nothingness, for she knew that He who is mighty could do great things in her and through her. She trusted. Once she said 'yes' to Him—[it was] finished. She never doubted."

"Do not be afraid to love Jesus tenderly. When you trust Him, He will do great things for you."

THOUGHT FOR THE DAY:
Confidence in God can do all things.

Ask for the grace to have an unshakable trust in God's power and love for you and for all.

Recite the "Prayer to Blessed Teresa."

Sixth Day:

True Love Is Surrender

" 'I thirst' has no meaning unless through total surrender I give all to Jesus."

"Today I will do whatever Jesus wants. And you will see that oneness. That surrender to God, to use you without consulting you. That accepting is a great sign of union with God. Holiness is that total surrender to God. *Totus tuus.* Completely yours. *Totus tuus.* Completely surrendered. Very clear! Complete. That accepting whatever He gives. That giving whatever He takes. You need much love to be able to see the hand of God."

"I only want to do what God wants. Let us have the courage to do what God wants, even if it is difficult."

"Often you see small and big wires, new and old, cheap and expensive, lined up. Unless and until the current passes through them, there will be no light. The wire is you and me. The current is God. We have the power to let the current pass through us, use us, and produce the Light of the World—Jesus; or refuse to be used and allow darkness to spread. Our Lady was the most wonderful wire. She allowed God to fill her to the brim, so by her surrender—'Be it done to me according to your word'—she became full of grace; and naturally the moment she was filled by this current, the grace of God, she went in haste to Elizabeth's house to connect the wire, John, to the current, Jesus."

THOUGHT FOR THE DAY:
Allow God to use you without consulting you.

Ask for the grace to surrender your whole life to God.

Recite the "Prayer to Blessed Teresa."

Seventh Day:
God Loves a Cheerful Giver

"Joy, to be fruitful, has to be shared."

"By this joy I mean that inner depth of joy in you, in your eyes, look, face, movements, actions, swiftness, etc. 'That My joy may be in you,' says Jesus. What is this joy of Jesus? It is the result of His continual union with God, doing the Will of the Father. 'I have come that my joy may be in you, and that your joy may be full.' This joy is the fruit of union with God, of being in the presence of God. Living in the presence of God fills us with joy. God is Joy."

"Joy shines in the eyes, comes out in the speech and walk...when people see the habitual happiness in

your eyes, it will make them realize they are the loved children of God."

"Without joy there is no love, and love without joy is not true love. And so, we need to bring that love and that joy into the world of today."

"Joy was the strength of Our Lady, too. Our Lady was the first Missionary of Charity. She was the first one to receive Jesus physically and to carry Jesus to others; and she went *in haste*. Only joy could give her this strength and swiftness to go and do the work of a handmaid."

THOUGHT FOR THE DAY:
We may not be able to give much, but we can always give the joy that springs from a heart that is in love with God.

Ask for the grace to find joy in loving and to share this joy with everyone you meet.

Recite the "Prayer to Blessed Teresa."

Eighth Day:
Jesus Made Himself the Bread
of Life and the Hungry One

"He proved His love to us by giving His own life, His own being. 'He being rich became poor' for you and for me. He gave Himself totally. He died on the Cross. But before He died, He made Himself the Bread of Life to satisfy our hunger for love, for Him. He said, 'Unless you eat My Flesh and drink My Blood, you cannot have life eternal.' And the greatness of that love of His made Him the hungry one, and He said, 'I was hungry and you fed Me, and unless you feed Me, you cannot enter eternal life.' That is the giving of Christ. And today God keeps on loving the world. He keeps on sending you and me to prove that He loves the world, that He still has that compassion for the world. It is we who have to be His love, His compassion in the world of today. But to be able to love we must have faith, for faith in action is love, and love in action is service. That is why Jesus made Himself the Bread of Life, that we might be able to eat and live and be able to see Him in the distressing disguise of the poor."

"Our life must be woven with the Eucharist. From Jesus in the Eucharist we learn how much God thirsts to love us and how He thirsts for our love and for the love of souls in return. From Jesus in the Eucharist we receive the light and strength to quench His Thirst."

THOUGHT FOR THE DAY:
Believe that He, Jesus, is in the appearance of Bread and that He, Jesus, is in the hungry, naked, sick, lonely, unloved, homeless, helpless, and hopeless.

Ask for the grace to see Jesus in the Bread of Life and to serve Him in the distressing disguise of the poor.

Recite the "Prayer to Blessed Teresa."

Ninth Day:
Holiness Is Jesus Living
and Acting in Me

"Our works of charity are nothing but the overflow of our love of God from within. Therefore, the one who is most united to Him loves her neighbor most."

"We must become holy not because we want to feel holy, but because Christ must be able to live His life fully in us."

"Sanctity is the acceptance of the will of God with a big smile…that's all. Just that acceptance, to accept Him as He comes in our life, accepting to take from us what He wants, to make use of us as He wants, to put us where He wants, to use us as He wants…without consulting us."

"Holiness is not in the feelings or in imagination, it is reality. One thing that helps me and will help you is this: works of love are works of holiness."

"Let us spend ourselves with Him and for Him. Let Him see with your eyes, speak with your tongue, work with your hands, walk with your feet, think with your head, and love with your heart. Is this not perfect union, a continual loving prayer? God is our loving Father. Let your light of love so shine before man that seeing your good works (the washing, sweeping, cooking, loving your husband and the children), they may glorify the Father."

"Be holy. Holiness is the easiest way to satiate Jesus's Thirst, His for you and yours for Him."

THOUGHT FOR THE DAY:
Charity for each other is the surest way to great holiness.

Ask for the grace to become a saint.

Recite the "Prayer to Blessed Teresa."

CONCLUSION

When Mother Teresa was asked to speak, she often repeated with firm conviction: "Holiness is not the luxury of the few, but a simple duty for you and for me." This sanctity is intimate love for and union with Christ: "The more tenderly you love, the more holy you become. Do not be afraid to love Jesus with your whole heart, whole soul, whole strength. His love is tender, immeasurable, if you only love Him and trust Him. Jesus has a special love for you."

Living in this intimate union with Jesus in the Eucharist and in the poor "twenty-four hours a day," as she would say, Mother Teresa became a true contemplative in the heart of the world. "Therefore, doing it with Him, we are praying the work—for in doing it with Him, doing it for Him, doing it to Him, we are loving Him. And in loving Him we come more and more into that oneness with Him, and we allow Him to live His life in us. And this living of Christ in us is holiness."

Radiating Christ

Mother Teresa's prayer "Radiating Christ," adapted from John Henry Cardinal Newman's "Meditations and Prayers," was one of her favorite ones. Since it beautifully expresses her desire to be intimately united to Jesus and to "give only Jesus" to others, she chose it as the first prayer to be recited each day after Holy Communion by the Missionaries of Charity.

Dear Jesus,
Help me to spread Your fragrance everywhere
   I go.
Flood my soul with Your Spirit and Life.
Penetrate and possess my whole being
So utterly that my life may only be
A radiance of Yours.

Shine through me and be so in me
That every soul I come in contact with
May feel Your presence in my soul.
Let them look up,
And see no longer me, but only Jesus!
Stay with me and then I will begin
To shine as You shine,
So to shine as to be a light to others.
The light, O Jesus, will be all from You;
None of it will be mine.
It will be You, shining on others through me.
Let me thus praise You
In the way You love best,
By shining on those around me.
Let me preach You without preaching,
Not by words but by example,
By the catching force,
The sympathetic influence of what I do,
The evident fullness of the love
My heart bears for You.
AMEN.

PHOTO CREDITS

page 18
Mother Teresa at the time she was awarded the 1979 Nobel Peace Prize. Calcutta, October 19, 1979. (© Kapoor Baldev/Sygma/CORBIS)

page 20
Mother Teresa visiting Dublin, Ireland, June 2, 1993. (© Polak Matthew/CORBIS SYGMA)

pages 30–31
Mother Teresa during her prayers at the Missionary of the Pure Heart in Calcutta, 1989. (© Raghu Rai/Magnum Photos)

page 35
Amid tight security, Mother Teresa gets a hug from an unidentified girl during a visit to Blessed Catharine Drexel Church, in Chester, Pa., Saturday, June 17, 1995. (AP Photo/Tim Shaffer, file)

page 39
Mother Teresa and Robert Morgan, on behalf of Youth Corps, release a dove as a symbol for peace in front of 20,000 people at Varsity Stadium, Toronto, Ontario, June 27, 1982. (© Bettmann/CORBIS)

page 45
A member of Mother Teresa's order with a child. India, 1979. (© Raghu Rai/Magnum Photos)

page 46
Calcutta, India, 1979. (AP Photo/Eddie Adams)